CAN YOU SEE WHAT I SEE?

CAN YOU SEE WHAT I SEE?

PICTURE PUZZLES TO SEARCH AND SOLVE

by Walter Wick

SCHOLASTIC INC.

New York   Toronto   London   Auckland   Sydney   Mexico City

New Delhi   Hong Kong   Buenos Aires

Published by Scholastic Inc.

SCHOLASTIC, CARTWHEEL BOOKS, and

associated logos are trademarks and/or

registered trademarks of Scholastic Inc.

Library of Congress

card catalog number: 2001049032

ISBN 0-439-16391-9

10 9 8 7 6 5 4 3 2 1   02 03 04 05 06

Printed in Mexico 49   First printing, March 2002

Book Design by Walter Wick and David Saylor

FOR LINDA

I would like to thank my studio manager, Daniel Helt, for his ever-expanding range of expert assistance in set building, photography, and computer graphics; my assistant, Kim Wildey, for her steady help and diligent management of the hundreds of props used for this book; and my wife, Linda, for her artistic wisdom and crucial advice on every aspect of this project.

A very special thanks to my editor, Grace Maccarone, for her unfailing support; to David Saylor for his excellent book design; to Bernette Ford, Jean Feiwel, and Barbara Marcus for their encouragement; to Edie Weinberg and Angela Biola for the trip to Buffalo; to Digicon Imaging, Inc., for the warm welcome; and to color expert Ronald Tubbs for generously sharing his trade secrets.

Contents

Can you see

what I see?

A silver sun,

a spotted dog,

a shiny cat,

a tiny frog,

a rolling pin,

six white mice,

a yellow top,

eleven dice,

a little camel

near a spring —

the only heart

inside the string!

Can you see
what I see?
A ladybug,
three stars of blue,
a piece of a jar,
a die showing two,
a marble Earth,
a crescent moon,
four baseball bats,
a fork and spoon,
a lobster claw,
a funny red bow,
a nut in a truck —
three jacks in a row!

Can you see
what I see?
A five-cent card,
a golden key,
a red game piece
on twenty-three,
a silver jack,
a yellow cone,
a floating flag,
a telephone,
seven horses,
fifteen hearts —
seven cards
with missing parts!

Can you see
what I see?
A dinosaur,
a sword, a swan,
a pair of horns,
a hippo yawn,
a blue kangaroo,
a boat, three planes,
a slithering snake,
a car, two trains,
a man in the moon,
a face on a sun,
a heart in a heart —
a hare on the run!

Can you see
what I see?
Two stars,
a screw,
an untied shoe,
seven rabbits,
a kangaroo,
a tool that's used
for rolling dough,
a squirrel that sits
where a pig should go,
a rolling rooster,
a rocking chair,
a two-piece duck —
a pop-out bear!

Can you see

what I see?

Five bowling pins,

a pencil,

a nail,

two black hats,

a lion's tail,

a tennis racket,

a lazy frog,

two cymbals,

three thimbles,

an obedient dog,

a domino cart,

a rolling ball —

the only clown

about to fall!

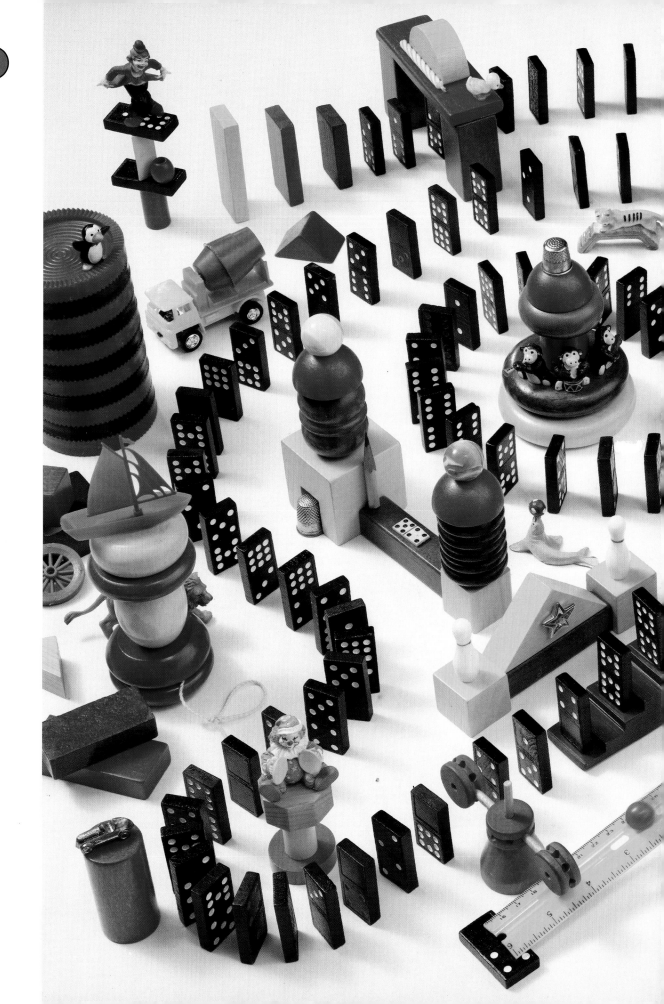

Can you see
what I see?
A man with an axe,
a girl with a broom,
a fisherman's basket,
a giant mushroom,
a tray of cakes,
two cats, a raccoon,
a path to a house,
a fork, knife, and spoon,
a wise old wizard,
a tower of bricks,
a king in a sling —
and six mirror tricks!

Can you see
what I see?
Two butterflies,
an anchor, a fish,
a baby bottle,
a steaming dish,
a chair, a panda,
a well-dressed goose,
binoculars,
three mice, a moose,
a truck on a hill,
a jack-in-the-box —
ten objects that match
ten pictures on blocks!

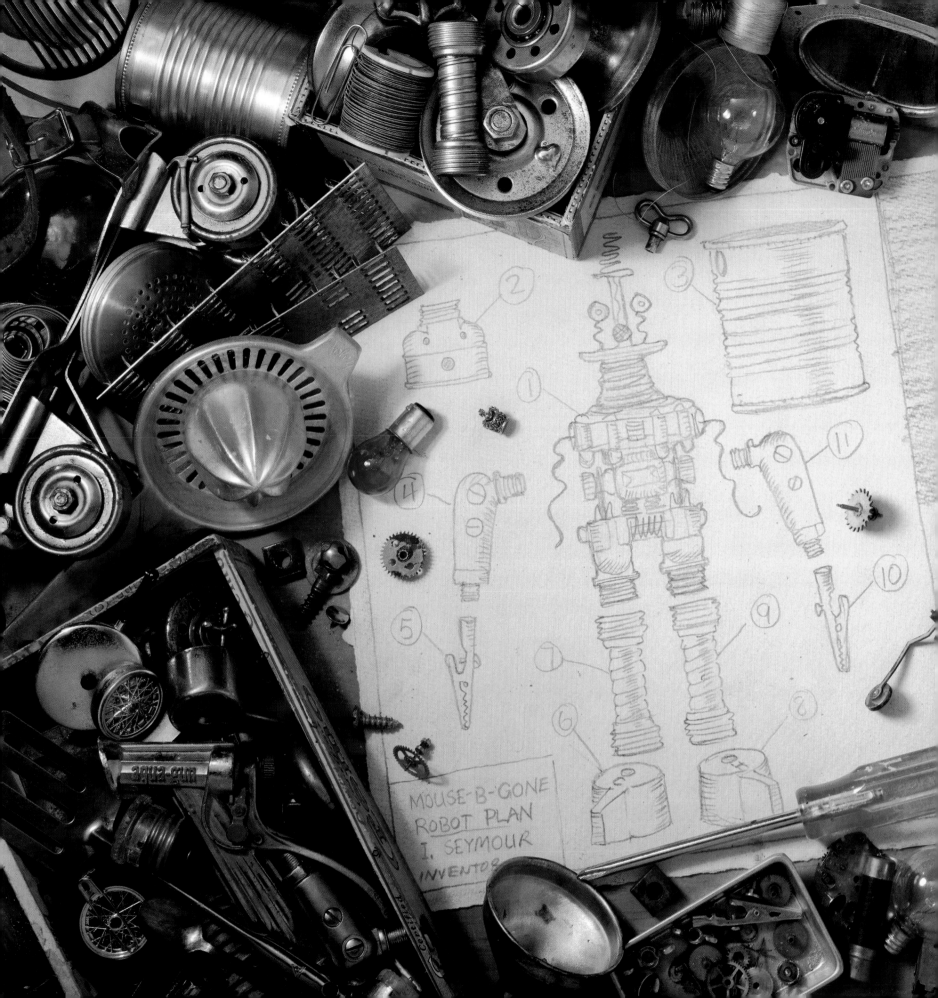

MOUSE-B-GONE
ROBOT PLAN
I. SEYMOUR
INVENTOR

Can you see

what I see?

A roller skate,

an old cruise ship,

a baseball glove,

a paper clip,

a jingle bell,

a water gun,

a frightened mouse

about to run,

a frying pan,

two silver hearts —

and all eleven

robot parts!

MOUSE VIEW

SIDE VIEW

Can you see
what I see?
A hot dog, a soda,
fries on the side,
a truck at the start
of a long bumpy ride,
nine yellow flags,
three arrows, a king,
a wagon, a web,
an ocean, a spring,
two tiger paws,
five camel humps —
get the EGGS
to the EXIT
crossing only
three bumps!

Can you see
what I see?
An apple, an acorn,
a magnet, a dart,
a toothbrush, a tub,
a one-wheeled cart,
three soldiers
with swords,
a marble, a mug,
an axe on a jack,
a bracelet, a bug,
four lanterns, a kite,
an upside-down tee —
an alphabet path
from A to Z.

Can you see
what I see?
Five planes,
a taxi,
a knot in a string,
a teapot spout,
a knight,
a king,
a bear with a bow,
a bear with honey,
two elephant trunks,
a sleeping bunny,
the kind of clock
that makes a noise —
now match ten parts
to ten broken toys!

Twenty-seven years ago, I got my first job in photography at a commercial studio. As the least experienced member of the staff, my job was to photograph objects that the other staff members thought were boring: sewing notions, fasteners, ball bearings, and various other bits of hardware. But I didn't think they were boring. I loved the challenge of getting the light and the shadows just right, and I delighted in making razor-sharp images that seemed almost as real as the objects.

Six years later I started my own studio. Seeking a subject matter more playful than the nuts and bolts of my earlier work, I made a series of photographs using colorful game pieces reminiscent of my childhood. Encouraged by an art director at *GAMES* magazine, I experimented with making a photograph that worked as a puzzle. With a few plastic toys, a number of small mirrors, and much trial and error, I created my first picture puzzle. I called it "The Amazing Mirror Maze," and it was published in *GAMES* in 1981.

For the next ten years I pursued a variety of photography assignments, ranging from illustrations for science publications to covers for paperback novels. But I also continued to create picture puzzles for *GAMES* magazine, always relishing the opportunity to work with its staff of game mavens and puzzle experts. Then, in 1991, I collaborated with writer/educator Jean Marzollo on a puzzle book for children called *I Spy: A Book of Picture Riddles*. The success of I Spy came as a complete surprise, and like Brer Rabbit in the briar patch, I was exiled to a place I loved—making picture puzzles—for another ten years, this time almost exclusively for the I Spy series.

Can You See What I See? marks a new chapter of the ongoing adventure in the briar patch. In this book, I seek to combine the classic, highly accessible search-and-find puzzle with other familiar types of puzzles. Observant readers will discover that each rhyme ends with the beginning of a new puzzle. Some of these "end games" are mazes, as in "Domino Effect," "Bump, Bump, Bump!," and "Alphabet Maze." "Picture Blocks," "Assembly Required," and "Spare Parts" are matching games. "Magic Mirror" and "Card Tricks" are forms of spot-the-difference games. ("Card Tricks" is inspired by a 1985 *GAMES* magazine puzzle devised by its editors.) "String Game" and "In Bins" are simple cryptic games. "See-Through" (a camouflage trick) and "Wood Shop" (an illusion) are both optical games. Hint: To see the bear "pop out," turn the book upside down. You may have to isolate the bear from the background with your hands or with paper to see the illusion.

The photographs were made with 8" x 10" and 4" x 5" view cameras using Ektachrome 64T film. The six mirror tricks in "Magic Mirror" were made by combining separate photographs on a computer. —Walter Wick

Walter Wick is the photographer of the I Spy books. He is author and photographer of *A Drop of Water: A Book of Science and Wonder*, which won the Boston Globe/Horn Book Award for Nonfiction, was named a Notable Children's Book by the American Library Association, and was selected as an Orbis Pictus Honor Book and a CBC/JNSTA Outstanding Science Trade Book for Children. *Walter Wick's Optical Tricks*, a book of photographic illusions, was named a Best Illustrated Children's Book by *The New York Times Book Review*, was recognized as a Notable Children's Book by the American Library Association, and received many awards, including a Platinum Award from the Oppenheim Toy Portfolio, a Young Readers Award from *Scientific American*, a *Bulletin* Blue Ribbon, and a Parents' Choice Silver Honor. Mr. Wick has invented photographic games for *GAMES* magazine and photographed covers for books and magazines, including *Newsweek, Discover*, and *Psychology Today*. A graduate of Paier College of Art, Mr. Wick lives with his wife, Linda, in New York and Connecticut.

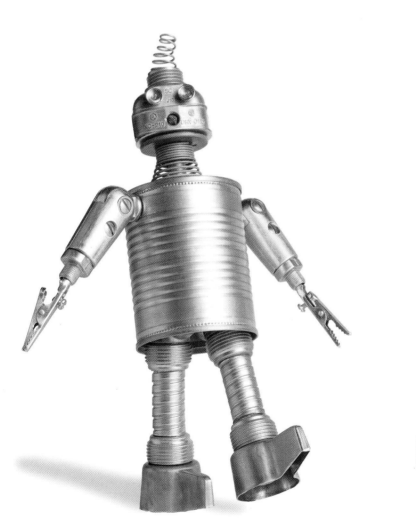